Handmade
Victorian Cards

Joanna Sheen

SEARCH PRESS

First published in Great Britain 2008

Search Press Limited
Wellwood, North Farm Road,
Tunbridge Wells, Kent TN2 3DR

Text copyright © Joanna Sheen, 2008

Photographs by Debbie Patterson, Search Press Studios

Photographs and design copyright © Search Press Ltd. 2008

ISBN-10: 1-84448-246-4
ISBN-13: 978-1-84448-246-7

The Publishers and author can accept no responsibility for any
consequences arising from the information, advice or instructions
given in this publication.

Readers are permitted to reproduce any of the items in this book
for their personal use, or for the purposes of selling for charity, free
of charge and without the prior permission of the Publishers. Any
use of the items for commercial purposes is not permitted without
the prior permission of the Publishers.

Suppliers

If you have difficulty in obtaining any of the materials and
equipment mentioned in this book, then please visit the
author's website: www.joannasheen.com
Alternatively visit the Search Press website for details of suppliers:
www.searchpress.com

Publisher's note

All the step-by-step photographs in this book feature
the author, Joanna Sheen, demonstrating how to make
Victorian greetings cards. No models have been used.

Dedication

To Pippa and Emily – who despite being very grown-up girls
now will always be little girls in my heart – with all my love.

Acknowledgements

I must thank everyone at Search Press for their help and
of course Debbie for the fabulous photography – what a
wonderful team to work with.

Thanks at this end to Pat Marsh for her help at the beginning,
middle and end of this project, and all the team here at
Joanna Sheen Ltd, particularly Sandra, Angela,
Gemma and Dave.

My biggest debt, however, has to be to Richard, my husband,
who for some unknown reason seems to be prepared to put
up with me crafting every waking hour and talking nothing
but card making for years now – I am so grateful to have the
best husband on earth – thank you!

Front cover
Child Carrying Blossom
*This lovely photograph is displayed behind a reproduction
Victorian photo mount and then accented with soft lacy
paper and organza ribbons. It is featured as the Fancy
Photograph project beginning on page 18.*

Page 1
Dainty Doily
*This pretty card combines printed lace papers with a small
paper doily and is topped with a Victorian scrap that was
printed out from a Victorian-themed CD set. The Dainty Doily
project begins on page 24.*

Contents

Introduction

I feel it is only fair to warn you from the very start that card making and crafting can become so addictive. My love for all things crafty has spanned my entire lifetime and is, I feel, the happiest hobby on earth.

My specific interest is in looking back to times and standards of craftsmanship gone by. I love the gentleness of the Victorian era and the belief, so embodied in Victorian crafts, that 'if it's worth doing, it's worth doing well'. I see no point in making a card that looks as though you have not bothered to take care with your craft. I make quick cards all the time, but you should always take that extra moment or two to make sure you really are giving something that can be treasured.

I hope you will take inspiration from the projects in this book and will enjoy applying them to your card making. You can follow a card exactly and make a replica, or you can use papers or embellishments that you happen to have in your workbox that will make your card unique.

The projects cover a variety of Victorian-inspired topics, from an oriental theme to babies, pansies and kittens! The cards manufactured in those days had so many small touches of extra care – and I try to do likewise with my cards. Pretty inserts add a little something to a card. If you have scraps left, why not decorate the back of the card with a strip of toning paper and a craft sticker. Make your cards as wonderful as the sentiments you are expressing and they will bring you not only more compliments but also more personal satisfaction in their creation.

Many of the projects used in this book feature toppers or backing papers printed out on a home inkjet printer from one of my Victorian-themed CDs. These are an invaluable source of images and ideas, but if you do not have a computer, there are lots of ready-printed decoupage sheets, backing papers and photographs available.

I hope you have many hours of fun both reading and using this book and I hope you find the Victorian style as addictive as I do!

Joanna Sheen

Opposite
A selection of greetings cards that you can make using the techniques shown in this book.

Materials

There are a few basic tools that all card makers should have by them. These should be the best quality you can afford, but there are also so many economy paths you can take. Never throw anything away – there is a real joy in making something from virtually nothing!

Basic materials

Cutting mat This protects whatever surface you are working on and provides an easily wipeable surface if you are cutting or stamping, colouring or gluing.

Tweezers These make many jobs far easier such as peeling the backing away from double-sided tape and picking up pressed flowers, beads or small embellishments.

You will need an assortment of sharp things. Crafters have different opinions as to which they prefer to use. I have used a **guillotine** for cutting cards and papers to size. You can also use a **craft knife** with a **metal ruler**. I have used **decoupage snips** for cutting out intricate shapes, but this can be done carefully using **scissors**.

Sticky products are another very subjective topic. I am a **double-sided tape** fan and use it constantly for sticking layers to cards. I use **silicone glue** for decoupage and for other jobs where I need to create a raised effect. I find the smaller tubes easier to handle. I use **latex-based white glue** rather than PVA glue with pressed flowers, as it rolls up in a small ball if you rub it gently and leaves no marks on cards, making it cleaner and easier to use.

A plastic **ruler** is useful for measuring and a **pencil** for marking.

Finally specialist extras. I thoroughly recommend the **Japanese screw punch**, a tool used originally by book binders to make deep holes. This makes it easy to make a hole through several layers of paper, card or even acetate anywhere on the card in a matter of seconds. You can also accumulate paper punches. I particularly like **corner punches** and use them to decorate the outer corners of card inserts.

Clockwise from top right: A cutting mat, metal ruler, guillotine, corner punch, double-sided tape, silicone glue, ruler, tweezers, latex-based white glue, scissors, decoupage snips, craft knife, pencil and Japanese screw punch.

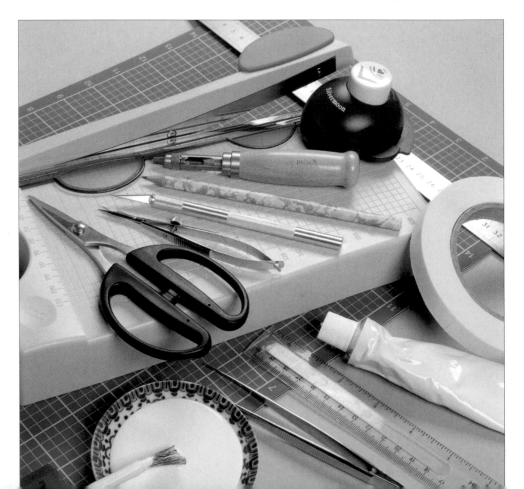

Card, paper and CDs for printing

The basic card blank should have a good weight. Do not be tempted to undermine your whole finished project with a flimsy base; I usually choose card blanks that are at least a 250gsm in weight.

I have used a whole variety of decorative backing papers, some available as pads of paper and some printed on a home printer from a Victorian-themed CD.

I have been involved in creating CDs for the craft market for several years now and they are a delightful way of housing a personal library of images, ideas and backing papers. Having a collection of craft CDs means you will have something to use for a card at any time of the day or night just by pressing the 'print' button. Take care when using CDs that you print out the finished item you wish to add to the card with care: set the print quality to 'photo' and use inexpensive photographic papers. The papers and toppers used in the projects in these books have all been printed on photographic papers with a pearl or satin finish, which means the images print really clearly and are as beautiful to look at as when they appear on the computer screen. You can also experiment with exciting mediums like inkjet acetate, vellums and unusual papers and see just how much more you can get out of the CDs.

Stamps and inkpads

There are rubber stamp addicts the world over, it is a craft that has been around for many, many years and shows no sign of any decrease in popular interest. The basic ingredients are a well-designed stamp, a good quality inkpad and a surface you want to decorate!

I personally opt for unmounted stamps as I need the space to store my ever-expanding collection of designs and images – I did warn you that crafting becomes an addiction! By using unmounted images, you can store ten times as many stamps and they are much more reasonable in price too. You use them by sticking them to an acrylic block.

Take time to get to know the various types of inkpad, as the effectiveness of your stamping will depend on this. A permanent inkpad is essential for stamping on acetate or vellum or if you want to watercolour over the image. I try to use a range of inkpads that are particularly designed to capture good detail, as many of the stamps I use are very intricate.

There are proprietary stamp cleaners available, which are very handy, particularly if you are using a permanent ink, but I also keep a pack of baby wipes (preferably alcohol free) beside me on my craft table to clean not only the stamp but me as well – stamping can get a little messy!

Embellishments

An embellishment is anything and everything that you can glue on to a card without it falling off in transit or when the card is handled! I am constantly amazed and delighted by the unique ideas I see on people's cards that make them really personal and individual.

The main embellishments I use are the standard things like ribbons (I particularly enjoy using organza ribbon), lace, brads and eyelets. I also add old photographs, tickets and other mementoes that either fit in with the theme of the card or mean something to the recipient. You can also use pressed flowers, paper flowers and of course gold and silver craft stickers. Acetate can be used both to showcase and to preserve pressed flowers on a card.

Opposite

Ribbon, lace, photo corner craft stickers, photographs, acetate, brads, pressed flowers and paper doilies, all used to embellish the cards in this book.

Making an insert

If you are using a dark-coloured base card for your project then it is very difficult to write a message inside and see it clearly, or you may just want to add a little extra touch of quality to the card. You may also need to hide the inside front of the card if your work shows through from the front. The easy answer to this is to make an insert. I generally use 100gsm paper (it can be more or less depending on what you have handy) and you can leave it plain, decorate it with a punch, stamp it or add craft stickers. There are also many CDs available that include inserts as part of the contents. I made an insert for each of the cards shown in this book.

1 To make this square insert, fold an A4 sheet of paper in half.

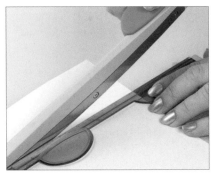

2 Trim it to square using a guillotine.

3 Take a corner punch and punch the outer corners, opposite the fold.

4 Attach double-sided tape to the front of the insert along the spine. The card will open better if the insert is attached only on the front in this way.

Lining an envelope

This is a little extra touch that is by no means essential, but if you are making a card for a particularly special occasion or want to add a bit of glamour, a lined envelope might fit the bill.

1 Take an envelope in the size you need and draw round it on the back of some patterned paper. Place the envelope against two of the ready-cut edges of the paper.

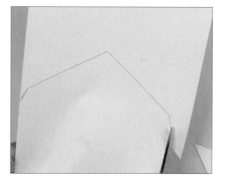

2 Cut out the evelope shape, cutting well within the lines.

3 Trim a little off each edge using a guillotine, so that your lining will fit easily in the envelope.

4 Slide the lining into the envelope and secure it using a glue stick or double-sided tape.

The card with its insert and a toning lined envelope.

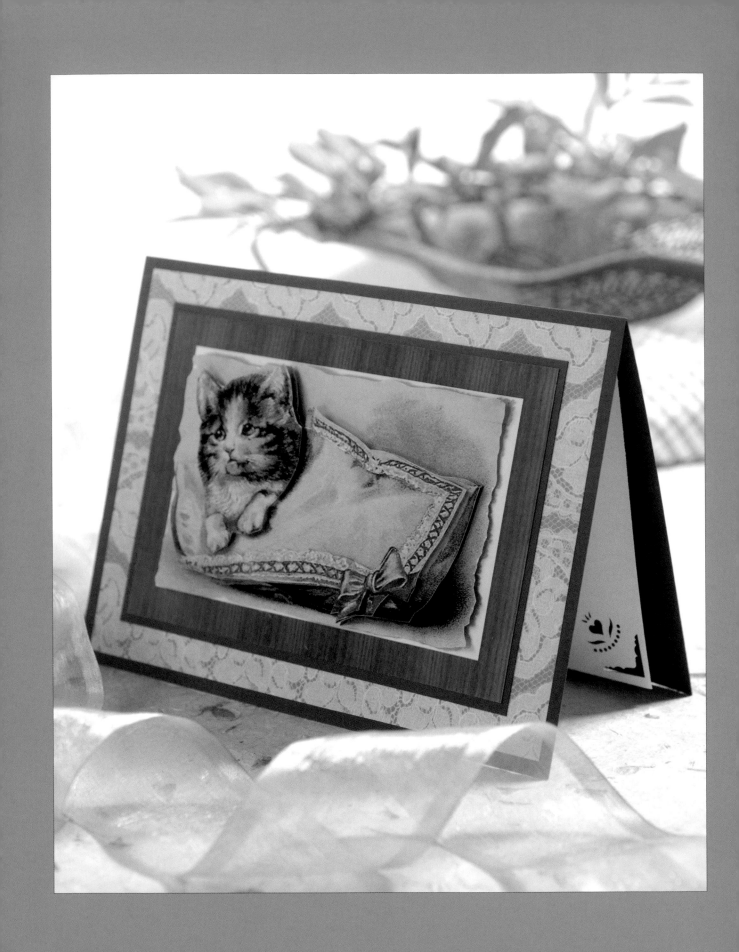

Decoupage Kitten

This beautiful kitten image is made into a pretty card using decoupage techniques that give the finished project an interesting three-dimensional effect. The images I used are printed from a Victorian-themed CD set and the lace paper is from a ready-printed pad, but you could choose your own alternatives.

YOU WILL NEED

Guillotine

Two sheets of A4 brown card

One sheet of lace paper

Decoupage kitten images

Double-sided tape

Silicone glue

Craft knife

Tweezers

Decoupage snips

1 Score and fold an A4 piece of brown card in half. Use a guillotine to trim the folded card to 20 x 14.7cm (7⅞ x 5⅞in). Also cut a piece of the same brown card to 16.5 x 11.4cm (6½ x 4½in).

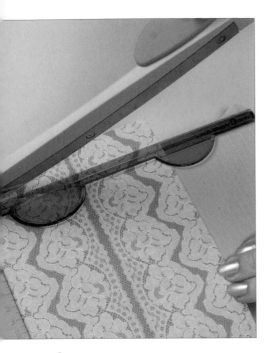

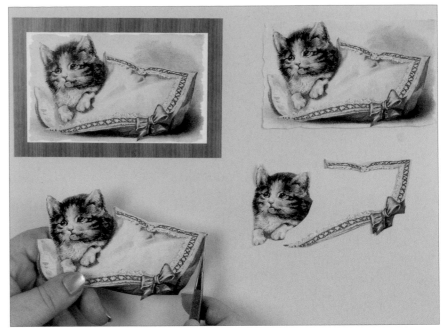

2 Cut the lace paper to 19 x 13.7cm (7½ x 5³/₈in).

3 Take the four kitten images and cut them out as shown, using decoupage snips.

4 Apply double-sided tape to the backs of the lace paper and the piece of brown card.

5 Peel off the backing from the double-sided tape and mount the lace paper and the brown card on the main card. Apply double-sided tape to the full kitten image and mount this on top.

6 Apply silicone glue to the back of the next kitten image (top right of step 3) and mount this on the card. Next, apply silicone glue to the back of the next image (bottom left of step 3). Use a craft knife to help you apply blobs of silicone glue. Always clean your craft knife immediately when using it with silicone glue, or use a cocktail stick instead.

7 Apply silicone glue to the backs of the final pieces and place these on the card using tweezers. Leave them to dry for at least half an hour and preferably overnight before putting the card in the post.

15

Exotic Birds

Birds are popular with both men and women, so this makes an excellent card for a whole range of people. The birds are decoupaged and the picture mounted on several layers of cool blue marbled papers. The black edges bring out the colours beautifully and add contrast to the overall design.

He's Bigger Than Me!

This delightful vintage image of two dogs makes a wonderful focal point and shows how effectively a Victorian image can be decoupaged. The colour toning of the marbled papers, gold and brown card gives a very satisfying result.

Fancy Photograph

Vintage photographs make superb subjects for cards. You can use a picture of a complete stranger just because it is beautiful or suits the message of the card, or if you are lucky enough to have a collection of old family photos, you can have one copied, save the originally carefully, and add the copy to your card. This image is from a bought set of Victorian photographs, and the lace paper is from a ready-printed pad. The flower frame was printed from a CD but you can also buy ready-printed Victorian album mounts. The flower design, lace paper and organza ribbon make this a deliciously feminine card.

YOU WILL NEED

Pink lace paper, 14.5 x 19.3cm (5¾ x 7⅝in)

Decoupage snips

Flower frame

Craft knife and cutting mat

Metal ruler

Printed photograph of girl

Maroon card blank, 14.3 x 20cm (5⅝ x 7⅞in)

Japanese screw punch or eyelet punch and hammer

Double-sided tape

Tweezers

Lilac organza ribbon

Scissors

Four gold photo corner craft stickers

1 Cut one side of the pink lace paper, following the lace pattern and using decoupage snips.

2 Cut out the centre of the flower frame using a craft knife, metal ruler and cutting mat.

3 Apply double-sided tape around the edges of the front of the photograph.

4 Mount the pink lace paper on the maroon card blank using double-sided tape. Mount the photograph and then the flower frame on top in the same way.

5 Open the card and place it on a cutting mat. Use a Japanese screw punch or an eyelet punch and hammer to make two holes for the ribbon. To use a Japanese screw punch, firmly press down into the layers of paper and card and allow the punch to twist and make the hole.

6 Use tweezers to push the end of the ribbon through the bottom hole from the inside of the card.

7 Push the other end of the ribbon through the other hole in the same way. Turn the card over and tie the ribbon in a bow. Trim the ends on the diagonal using sharp scissors.

8 Take four photo corner craft stickers, peel off the backing and place them using tweezers at the corners of the flower frame.

My Best Friend and I

*This pretty vintage image is one that will please a wide variety of recipients
and the colours of the sepia-toned photograph blend beautifully with the old
Victorian lettering and the marbled papers.*

Congratulations!

This illuminated frame has been carefully cut out and a Victorian man's photograph inserted, which together with the calligraphy-style paper and scroll would make a great card to celebrate a young man's achievement.

Dainty Doily

Victorian scraps are available already pre-cut, or you can print them out from a CD. Here a basket of flowers is very effectively showcased on a variety of lacy backgrounds from a ready-printed pad. The flower basket has been attached to the card with silicone glue, so it is nicely raised off the card to create extra interest.

YOU WILL NEED

Guillotine

Black and white, green and pink lace papers

Double-sided tape

Black card blank, 14.7 x 14.7cm (5¾ x 5¾in)

Paper doily

Silicone glue

Craft knife

Flower basket image

Decoupage snips

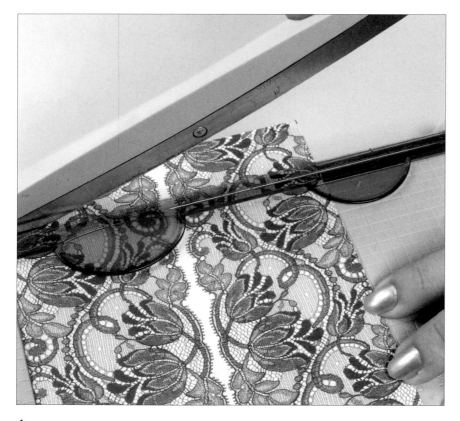

1 Cut all the lace papers to size using a guillotine: the black and white paper should be 13.8 x 13.8cm (5⅜ x 5⅜in); the green should be 11 x 11cm (4⅜ x 4⅜in); and the pink should be 10 x 10cm (4 x 4in).

2 Apply double-sided tape to the backs of the lace papers. Mount the black and white paper on the black card blank, and the green paper centrally on top.

3 Mount the pink lace paper diagonally in the centre of the card.

4 Apply silicone glue to the back of the paper doily, using a craft knife or a cocktail stick. If you use a craft knife, clean it straight away.

5 Cut out the flower basket image using decoupage snips.

6 Mount the paper doily on the card, then apply silicone glue to the flower basket image and mount this in the centre. Leave to dry for several hours, and preferably overnight, before sending.

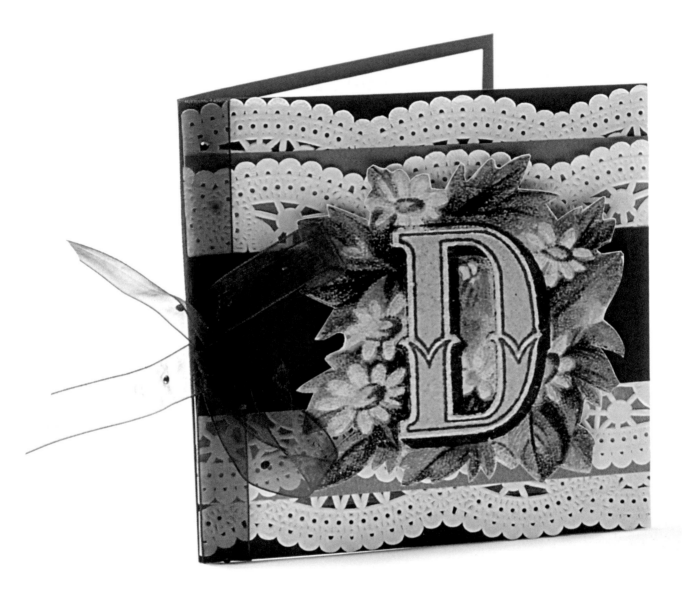

D for Diana

A decorated initial instantly personalises this card, and mixing the vintage image with layers of lace and an organza bow is very effective.

An Angel in Green

This beautiful child is decorated by circles of lace to echo the shape of the Victorian scrap and then mounted on to layers of coordinating colours.

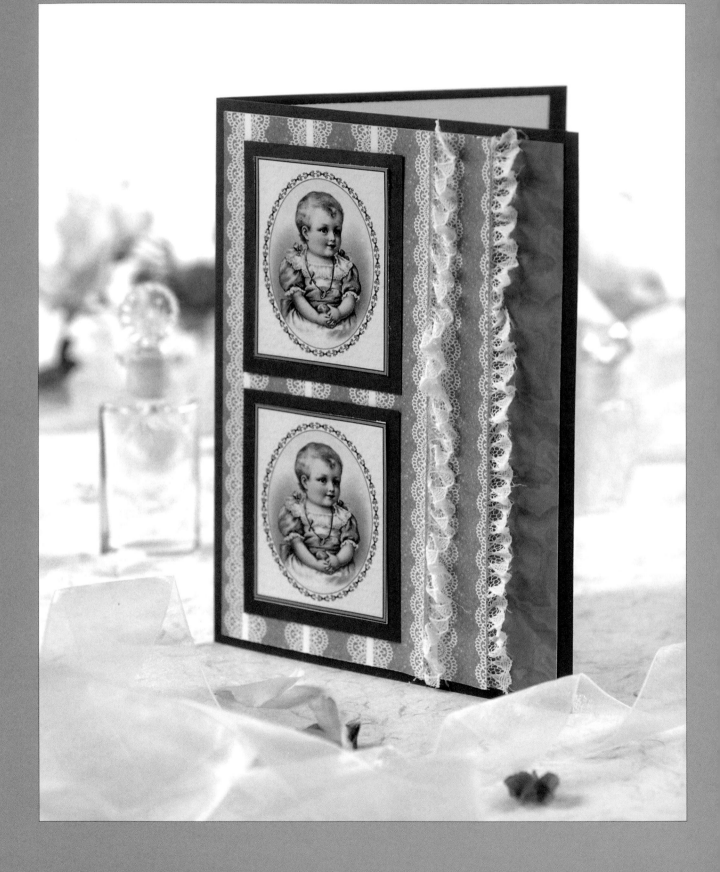

Baby Lace

One of the happiest times to celebrate is the arrival of a new baby. Mothers are often deluged with cards and flowers, gifts and callers. By making your own card rather than buying a ready-made one, you will make sure that the new mum has not only a card that is completely unique but also something she can keep and treasure forever.

The baby image and matching backing papers used here were printed from a Victorian-themed CD set, but you can choose your own.

YOU WILL NEED

Guillotine

One sheet of purple marbled paper

Two sheets of lined pink lace paper

Narrow 15mm (5/8in) ruffled lace

Double-sided tape

Scissors

Sheet of maroon card

Two baby images

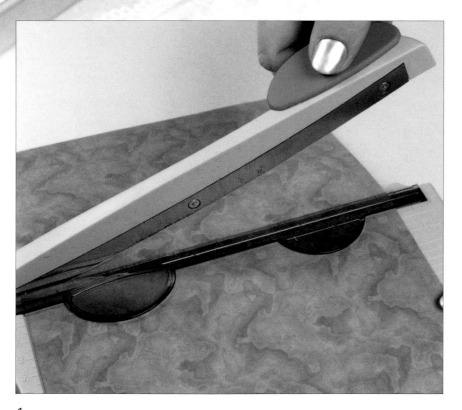

1 Use the guillotine to cut the papers to size. Cut the purple marbled paper to 13.6 x 19cm (5³/₈ x 7½in); then cut the two pieces of lace paper to 8.6 x 19cm (3³/₈ x 7½in) and 11 x 19cm (4³/₈ x 7½in).

2 Apply double-sided tape all round the back of the lace papers and remove the backing. Stick down a strip of ruffled lace on one long edge of each piece, so that the frilled edge of the lace will show from the front. Trim the lace to size.

3 Cut out the baby images. Use the guillotine to cut two pieces of maroon card, 6.5 x 8.4cm (2½ x 3⁵/₁₆in).

4 Mount the baby images on the maroon cards using double-sided tape. Mount the lace papers on to the maroon card blank, the widest first.

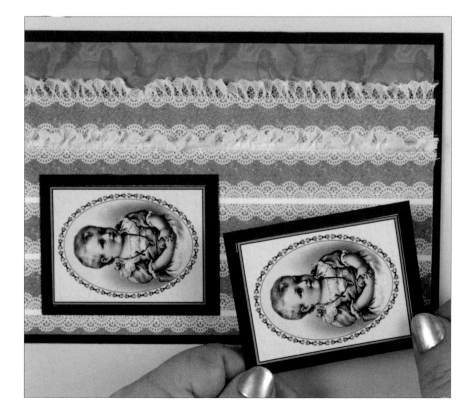

5 Mount the baby pictures on to the narrower piece of lace paper using double-sided tape.

Golden Baby

Wide ivory and grey lace has been wrapped around the layer of gold card and held with tape before layering on to the main card. A family baby photograph would work very successfully here too.

Baby Dreaming

The daisy design is actually a piece of decorated voile fabric, which I wrapped around a pale green piece of card. I fixed this at the back with double-sided tape and attached ruffled lace around the edge before finally attaching that layer to the base card.

Pansy Duet

Pressed flowers lend themselves perfectly to card making as they are obviously completely flat and, when covered with acetate like this, they last for many years and make a treasured keepsake. In the language of flowers, pansies mean sentimental thoughts or 'thinking of you', and so they are ideal if you are making a card for a special person.

The lace and calligraphy papers used here came from ready-printed pads. You can of course choose your own to complement the pressed flowers.

YOU WILL NEED

Guillotine

One sheet of green lace paper

One sheet of calligraphy paper

Green card blank, 14.5 x 14.5cm (5¾ x 5¾in)

Double-sided tape

Pressed flowers

Latex-based white glue

Tweezers

One sheet of acetate

Japanese screw punch or eyelet punch and hammer

Cutting mat

Four gold-coloured brads

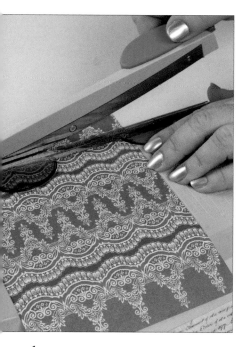

1 Use the guillotine to cut the papers to size. The green lace paper should be 11 x 11cm (4⅜ x 4⅜in); the larger calligraphy paper should be 13.5 x 13.5cm (5⅜ x 5⅜); and the smaller one should be 7.5 x 7.5cm (3 x 3in).

2 Apply double-sided tape to all the papers. Stick the larger calligraphy paper on to the green card blank.

3 Stick all the papers in place and use tweezers to place the pressed stalks and flowers.

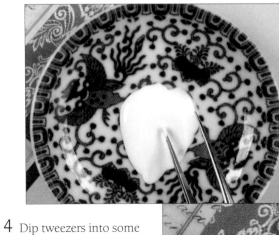

4 Dip tweezers into some latex-based white glue (not PVA glue). Slide the tweezers under the pressed flowers and stalks to stick them down. Latex-based glue will dry clear so will not show. An alternative to using the tweezers is to slide a little glue on a cocktail stick under the flowers.

5 Cut the acetate to the same size as the larger of the pieces of calligraphy paper: 13.5 x 13.5cm (5³/₈ x 5³/₈). Place it over the card.

6 Open the card and place it on a cutting mat. Use the Japanese screw punch or an eyelet punch and hammer to make four holes through the acetate, papers and card front as shown.

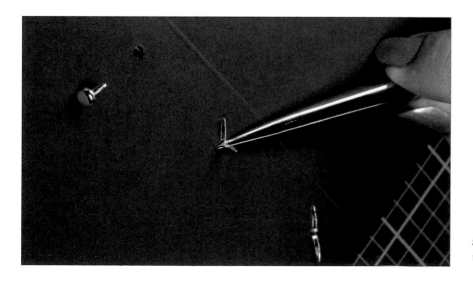

7 Push the brads through the holes and separate the backs using tweezers to secure them.

A Vase of Flowers

This same idea can be used with many different shapes or papers to make the vase.
You could also stamp a vase, make a plain vase from card and decorate it with
craft stickers, or just use a suitable Victorian scrap.

Roses and Metal Leaf

Here the backing paper has been decorated with flashes of gold and copper leaf, to add to the vintage, distressed effect of the card.

Oriental Elegance

Cards with an oriental theme have long been a favourite of mine and indeed this theme runs through many original Victorian designs. Here stamping and paper weaving are combined to make an intricate and subtle card that will give real pleasure to the recipient. The papers come from a blue and white ready-printed pad to complement the stamped image.

1 Stick the bamboo design rubber stamp on to the acrylic block. Leave the stamp lying flat and tap the midnight blue inkpad on to it to ink it.

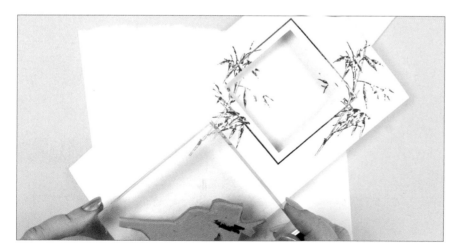

2 Take the white card blank and place scrap paper inside to protect the aperture area. Stamp the card randomly as shown.

YOU WILL NEED

Midnight blue solvent inkpad

Bamboo design rubber stamp

Acrylic block for stamping

Ginger jar design rubber stamp

Scrap paper

White aperture three-fold card blank, 13.5 x 24.7cm (5¼ x 9¾in)

Two sheets of white card

Instant drying majestic blue pigment inkpad

Decoupage snips

Guillotine

Three different printed blue patterned sheets

Double-sided tape

Tweezers

Silicone glue

3 Ink the ginger jar stamp with the instant drying majestic blue pigment inkpad and stamp the design on to a white sheet of card.

4 Cut out the ginger jar design using decoupage snips.

5 Use the guillotine to cut 1cm (³⁄₈in) wide strips from the three different printed sheets.

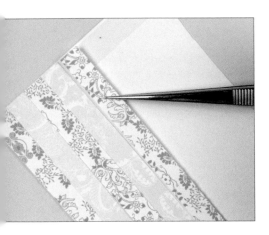

6 Cut a sheet of white card to 9 x 11cm (3½ x 4¼in). Apply a strip of double-sided tape at the top and peel off the backing. Choose strips from two of the patterned papers and use tweezers to stick them alternately across the piece of card.

7 Take strips from the third patterned paper and weave them in and out of the first strips, going under, over, under, over and so on. Leave a strip's width between each.

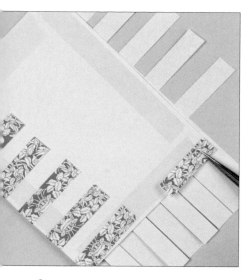

8 Turn the woven artwork over and apply double-sided tape to the edges of the back. Peel off the backing and use tweezers to fold over the strips to secure them.

9 Apply double-sided tape to the back of the completed woven artwork. Place the artwork behind the aperture of the three-fold card blank as shown. Then fold over the flap so that it sticks to the woven artwork in the right position.

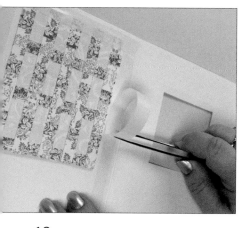

10 Open up the flap again with the woven artwork in place. Apply double-sided tape around the edges of the flap and peel off the backing. Fold over the flap again so that it sticks to the back of the aperture flap.

11 Apply silicone glue to the back of the ginger jar and place it on the card.

Brushing Her Hair

This wonderful image of a small girl brushing her hair is mounted on a background of woven papers with sunflowers and lace mixed together and photo corners have been added for emphasis.

Marbled Cat

The cat image is so strong that it is enough merely to stamp it in sepia without further colouring. The picture is mounted on a card decorated with woven paper strips of warm-coloured marbled papers.

Index

This is a typically Victorian image of a beautiful child, decorated by paper doilies like the Dainty Doily card on page 24 and mounted on to layers of coordinating colours.